My Michigan Summer

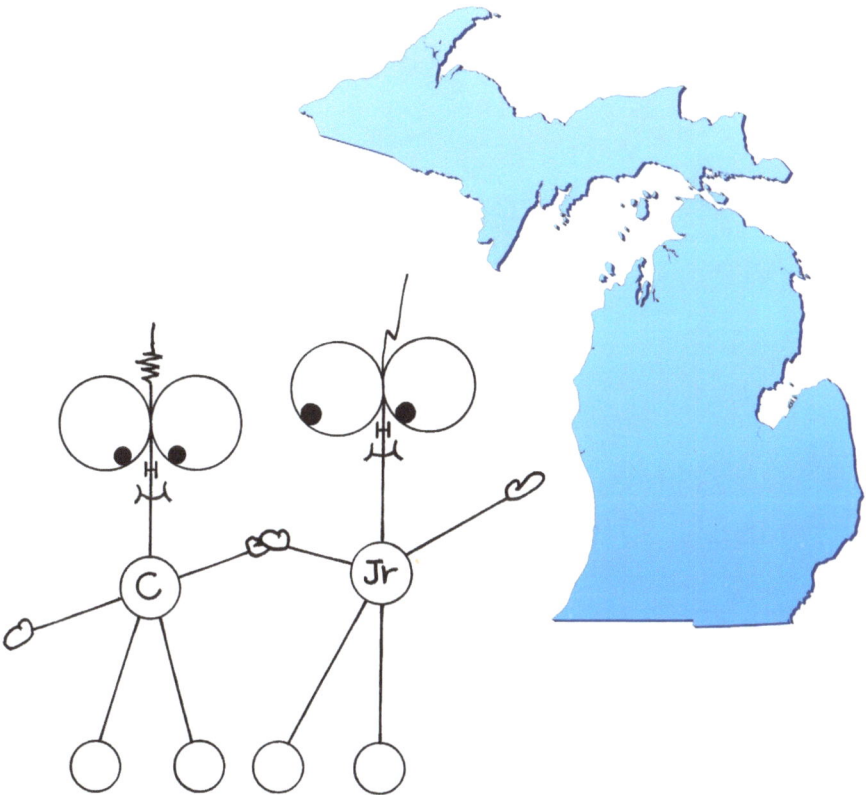

Written by Rose Klopf Tithof

Illustrated by Frederick Paul Arndt

ISBN: 978-0-9891006-0-1 (ebook)
ISBN: 978-0-9891006-1-8 (paperback)

To my Grand "Bubbies"
Lair, Truman, Lawrence, and Berlin–
the original
California and Michigan kids.
Love, MiMi
—RKT

To my Grand Nephew, Charlie,
whose name was the inspiration for
the character "Charlie" in this book.
—FPA

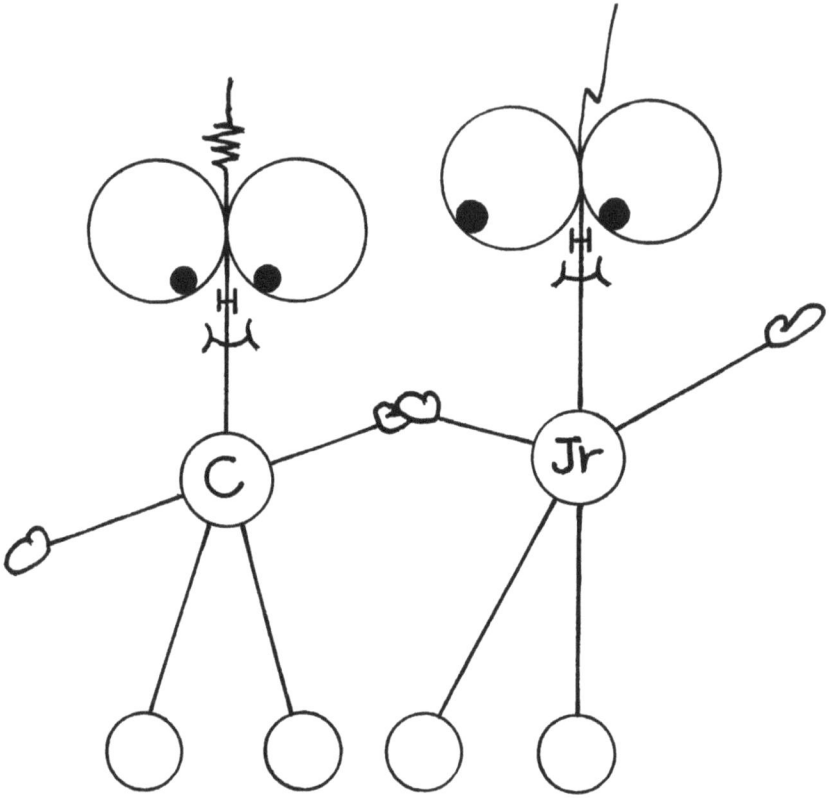

Charlie and **Junior** are cousins who live over 2,000 miles apart.

Even though they have only been together once, they feel in their hearts **they'll always be buddies** no matter how much distance is between them.

Charlie lives in the big city of
Los Angeles, California.

Junior lives in the small town of
Chesaning, Michigan.

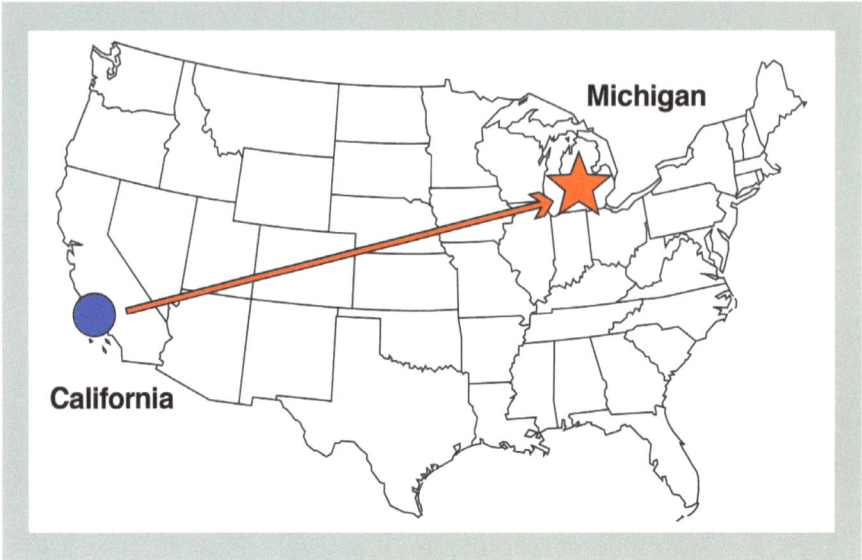

Charlie plans to spend his summer vacation at Junior's home in Michigan.

He tells his mom, "I can't wait to be with Junior, but it will be a **little scary** being so far away from home."

Charlie's mom comforts him, "Everyone is a little afraid of new places...

it's ok, Charlie."

Soon Charlie is in Michigan.

"Yeah, Charlie! I'm so excited you're here," calls Junior. "Come on, let's play in my yard."

"Wow, this yard is huge. There are so many trees. Are there any wild animals here?" Charlie asks, eyes wide.

With a smile to comfort his cousin, Junior says, "There's nothing dangerous...

it's ok, Charlie."

Junior shouts as he jumps into his small electric car, "Charlie! Come on. Let's go for a ride."

"Ohhh, Junior! I've never ridden in one of these. Don't go too fast."

"I won't...

it's ok, Charlie."

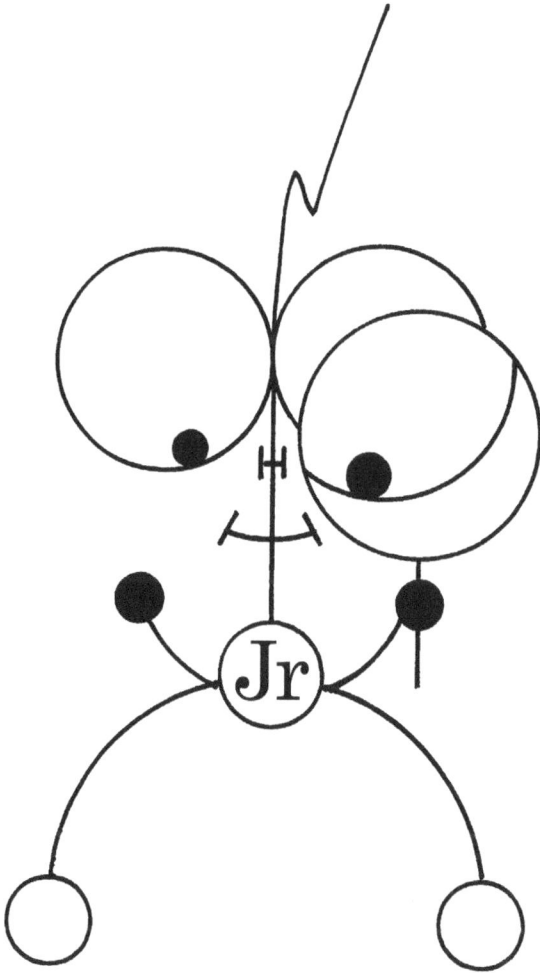

While in Junior's backyard, the boys notice lots of bugs.

"Charlie, check out how this ladybug looks so big through my magnifying glass."

"We don't have as **many different kinds of bugs** in my yard at home," Charlie says.

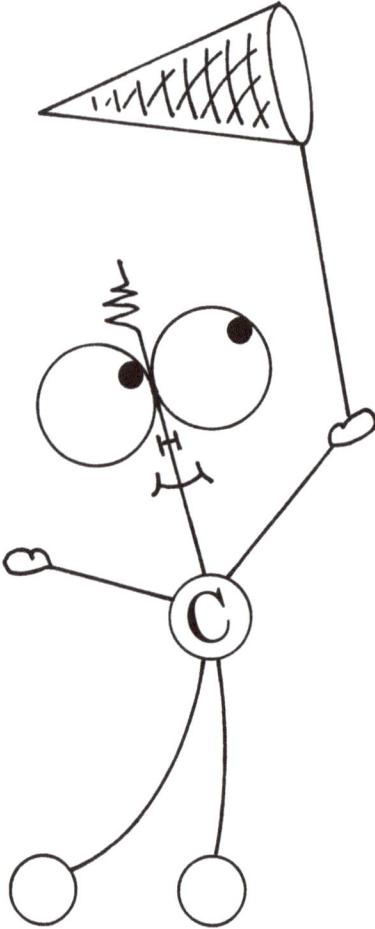

"Hey, Junior, look quick! I see a **monarch butterfly.** We have these in California too. I like seeing something from home."

Junior's parents take the boys to visit his uncle's farm.

As the boys walk by a cornfield, Charlie says nervously, **"This field is big, and the corn is way above my head. We could get lost in there."**

Junior answers, "Right, we won't go in...

it's ok, Charlie."

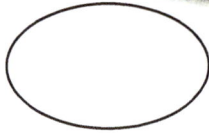

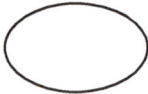

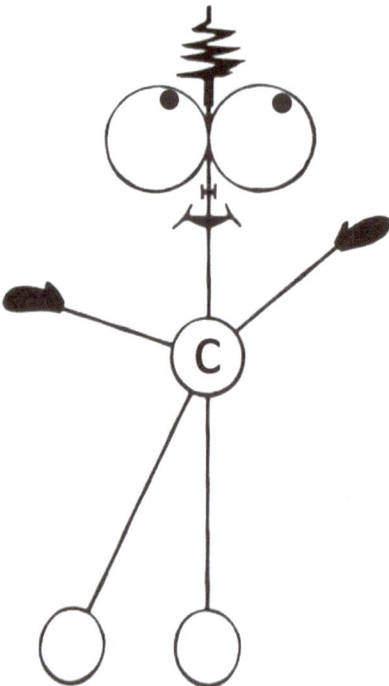

"In my neighborhood in Los Angeles, we have a **community garden** where my family and neighbors share a place to plant. It's **REALLY little** compared to the huge fields here," Charlie says.

Down the road from the farm, Charlie is surprised, **"What are those tall towers?** They look like giant space ships."

Junior explains, **"They're grain storage silos.** That's where they put corn after it's harvested."

"This is fun. I think I like being in Michigan," Charlie says.

Later that day, Junior learns that his parents plan to take the boys on a trip to see **Northern Michigan.**

As they drive north, Charlie says, **"I feel like I'm riding through a forest.** There are so many trees, and the leaves are thick and green."

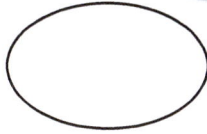

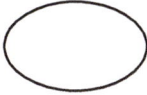

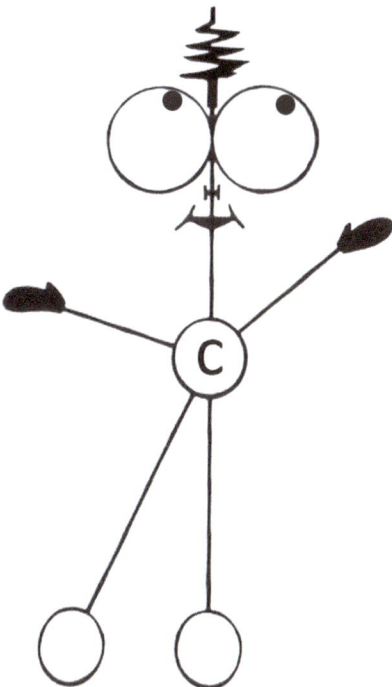

"Back home in Los Angeles, we have palm trees that are tall and skinny. Most of the green is at the top."

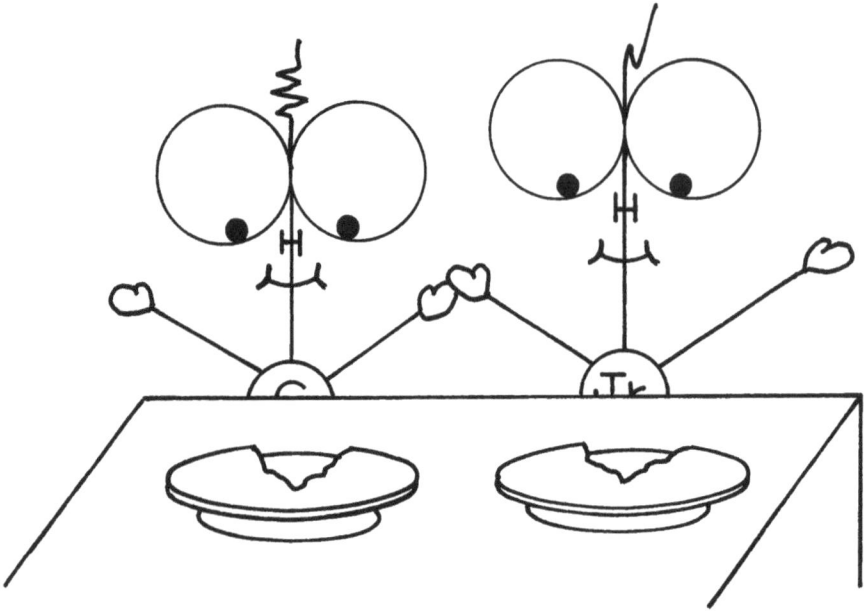

The first stop on their trip north is **Traverse City.** The boys enter a cherry pie-eating contest at the annual **Cherry Festival.**

Junior and Charlie love the pies.

"Yummmm."

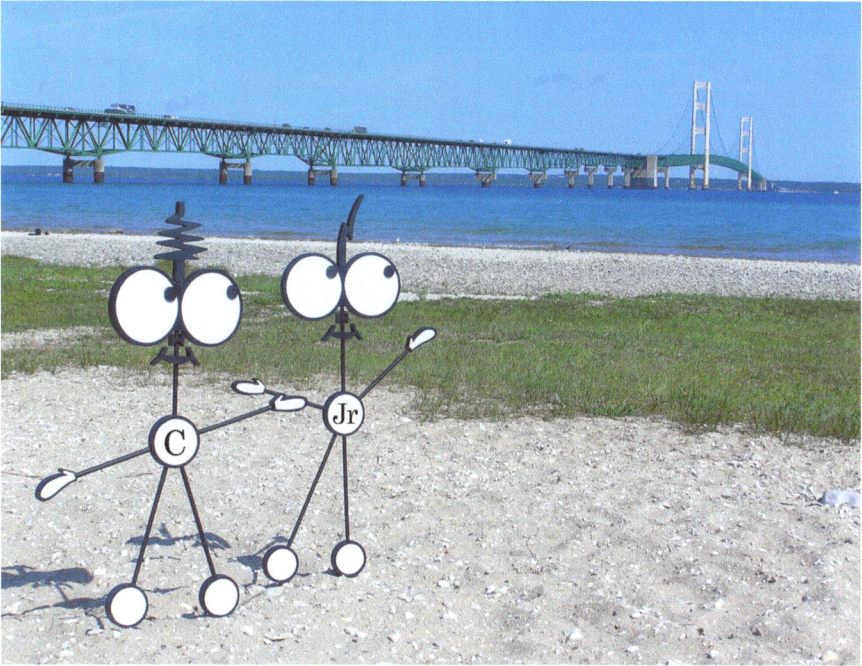

The next stop on their trip is Mackinaw City.

Junior and Charlie run to the shore of Lake Huron to see the **Mackinac Bridge.**

"It's HUGE," yells Charlie. "I've never seen a bridge this big before."

"The Mackinac Bridge is at the Straits of Mackinac where Lake Michigan and Lake Huron come together," says Junior.

Using his hands, Junior shows Charlie how to make the shape of the **State of Michigan.**

"It looks like two mittens!" Junior says.

Junior's parents and the boys head off to **Mackinac Island.**

"We'll have to take a ferry boat to get to the Island. It's so fun to see everything from the top deck," says Junior.

The boys love the fast boat ride.

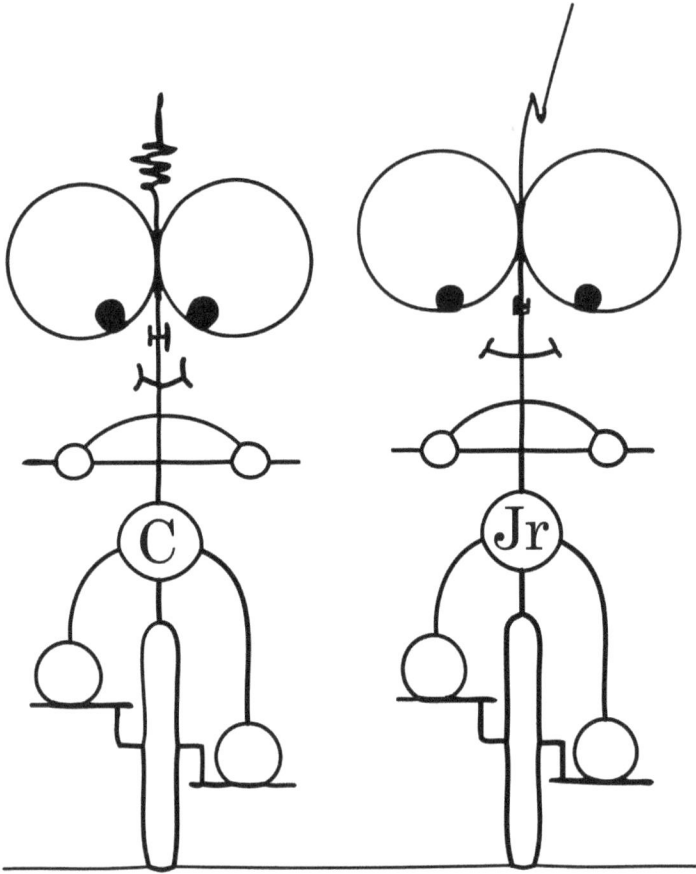

On Mackinac Island, **Junior and Charlie ride rental bikes** along the trail next to the lake.

"Doesn't it feel like we're living a long time ago?" Junior asks as they watch the horses and buggies going by.

Continuing their trip north, Junior's parents take the boys to the small town of Grand Marais in Michigan's Upper Peninsula. They walk through the woods to see Sable Falls.

"Wow, this river really moves fast. I'm afraid we might fall in!" says Charlie.

"We'll go back to the walking trail...

it's ok, Charlie."

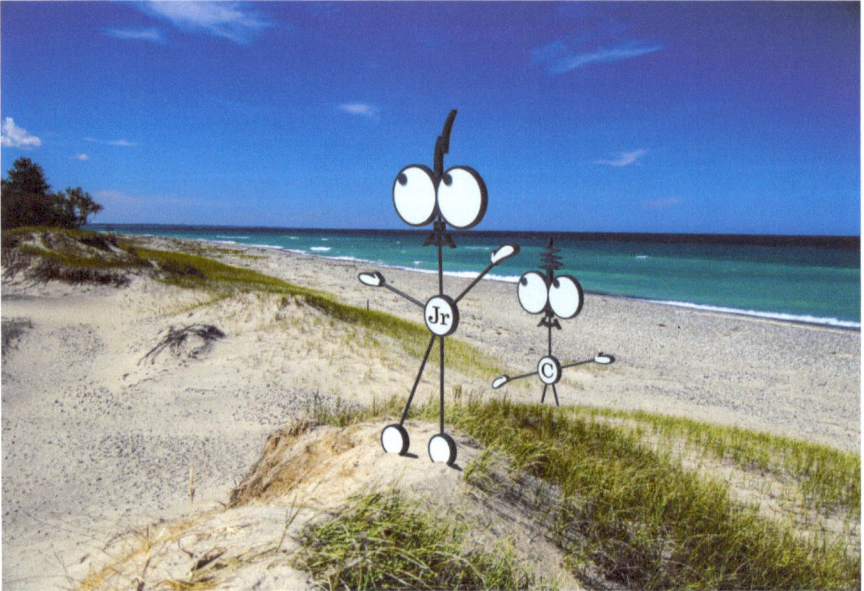

Junior and Charlie play at Agate Beach on the **shore of Lake Superior.**

Charlie calls out to Junior, "It seems like we have the whole beach to ourselves!"

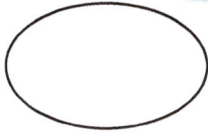

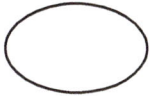

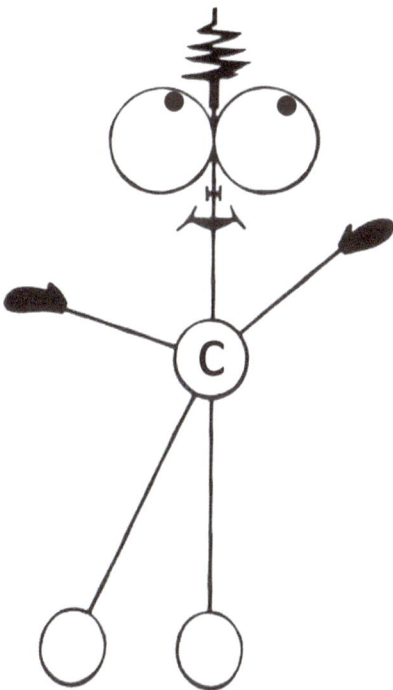

"Being in Northern Michigan is so different from where I live in California. The beaches back home can be crowded," says Charlie.

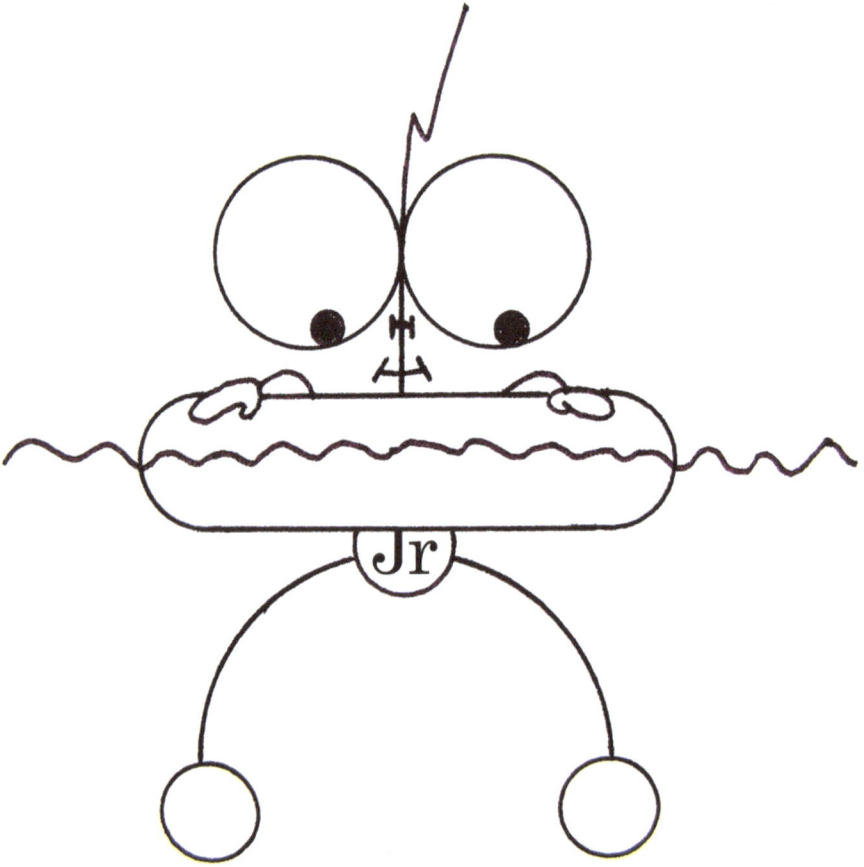

"Let's go in the water, Charlie," Junior says as he grabs an inner tube.

Charlie runs in and gets water in his mouth. He calls out in surprise, "This **water doesn't taste salty** like when I swim in the ocean."

Junior laughs, "In Michigan our lakes are **just plain, fresh water.**"

Soon **rain clouds** roll in over the lake.

Charlie is a little frightened again, "We don't have clouds like these very often in Los Angeles. These are so big and dark. The sun almost always shines at my house."

Junior says, "It's just going to rain, but we should head for the car...

it's ok, Charlie."

Before long, the boys are back on the road to Junior's home in Chesaning, but their **memories of Northern Michigan will last a lifetime.**

Back in Chesaning, Charlie and Junior decide to camp in a tent in the backyard.

"Hey, Junior, I really like being in your yard now," Charlie says bravely. **"I can't wait to sleep in the tent."**

That night the boys huddle in the tent. **Soon they hear loud noises outside the tent,** and they run to the house and into the arms of Junior's parents.

"What are those noises?" the boys ask, breathlessly.

Junior's parents reassure them, "You probably only heard an owl or a dog, nothing to be afraid of."

With a hug and a smile, Junior's parents say, "Don't be afraid. We are here in the house with the windows open so you can call to us anytime...

it's ok, Charlie...

it's ok, Junior."

Finally, both boys are tucked into their sleeping bags.

"I'm really glad I spent my summer vacation with you, Junior," Charlie says with new confidence.

"Different is cool — not scary anymore."

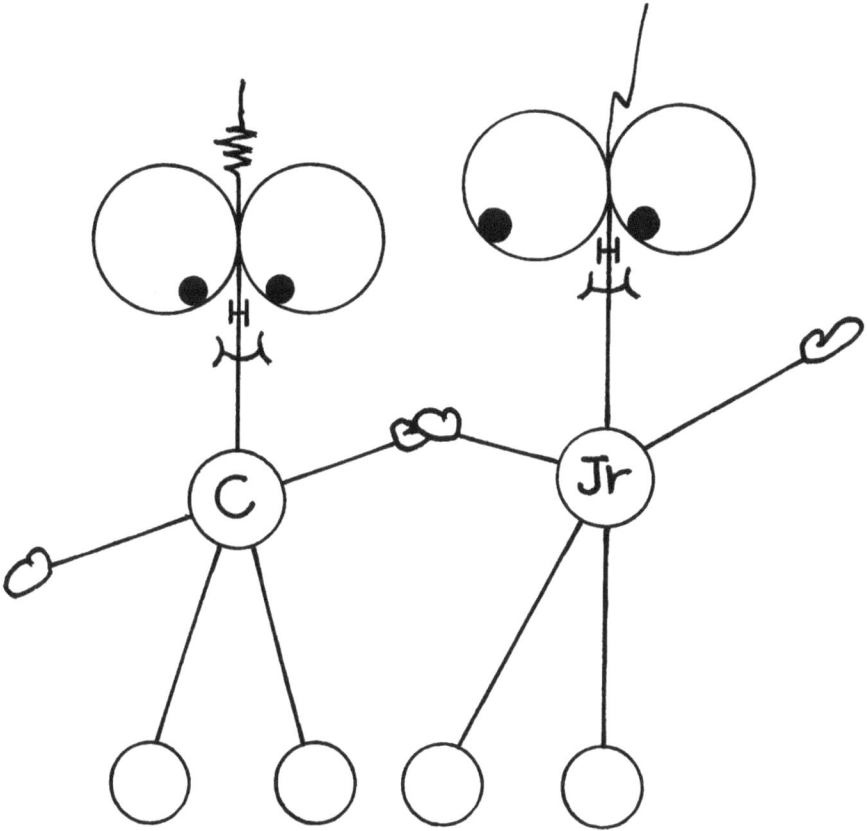

It's time for Charlie to go back to Los Angeles.
Junior says, "Good-bye, Charlie. I'm going to
miss you."

"Ohhh, I am going to miss you too," says
Charlie.

Even though they will be apart, both know
they will always be best buddies.

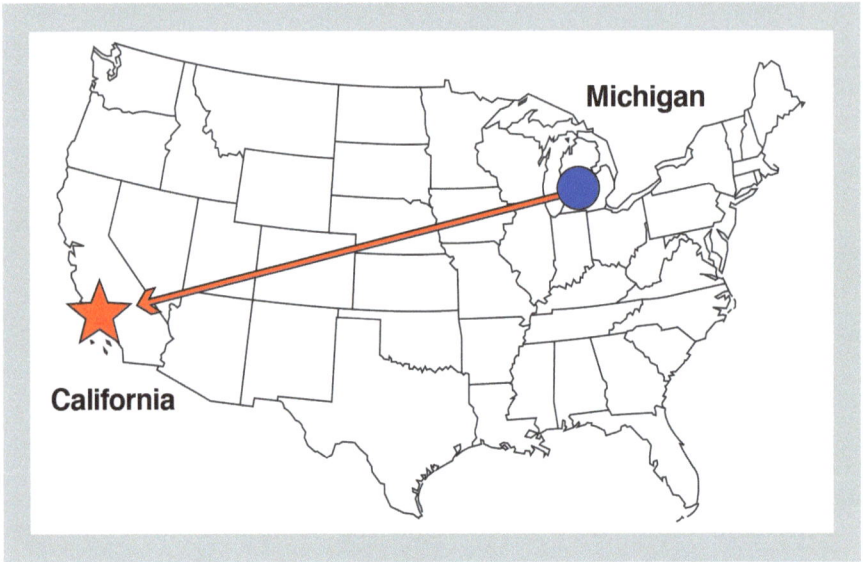

Soon Charlie is on his way back to California.

Back in Los Angeles, Charlie thinks, "I'd like to have Junior visit me next summer. **I bet I could show him lots of new things too.**"

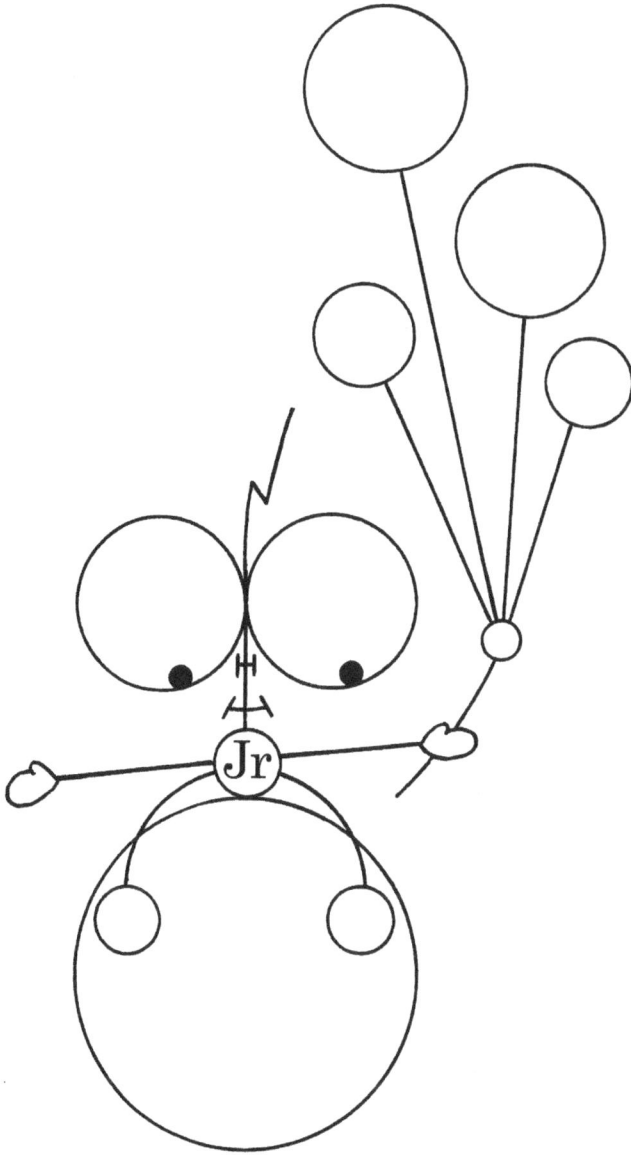

Back in Michigan, Junior thinks...

"Los Angeles here I come!"

Junior and Charlie's Michigan Scrapbook

Fort Michilimackinac
Mackinaw City, MI

Michigan State Capitol
Lansing, MI

Grand Haven Pier
Grand Haven, MI

Curwood Castle
Owosso, MI

Lumberman's Monument
Iosco Co., MI

Spartan Stadium
Michigan State University
East Lansing, MI

Michigan Stadium
University of Michigan
Ann Arbor, MI

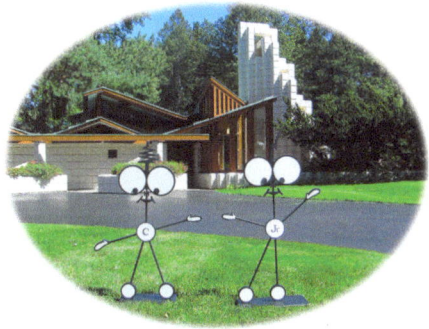

Alden Dow Home & Studio
Midland, MI

Credits

Photo Credits

Santa Monica Bch © Kazmaniac/Dreamstime.com

California Palm Tree © Tommyschultz/Dreamstime.com

Los Angeles Downtown © Roza/Dreamstime.com

Community Garden © Alisonh29/Dreamstime.com

Au Sable Lighthouse © Rudi1976/Dreamstime.com

Michigan Silos © PattyB154/Dreamstime.com

Monarch Butterfly © Ambientideas/Dreamstime.com

American Roads U.P. © Picturemakesllc/Dreamstime.com

Michigan Map © Skvoor/Dreamstime.com

Lake Superior Bch © Ehrlif/Dreamstime.com

Country Road © Saddako123/Dreamstime.com

Other Credits

Charlie and Junior Wood Models – Bemiss Creative Concepts

Photography – Frederick Arndt Artworks

Chesaning, Michigan © Ken (Sentrawoods) - http://www.flickr.com/photos/sentrawoods/2643488639/, CC BY-SA 2.0, https://commons.wikimedia.org/w/index.php?curid=28079138

Rose (Rosalee) Klopf Tithof — Author

Rosalee Klopf Tithof is now enjoying her hobby of writing children's stories after retiring from her rewarding years as an English teacher. She earned her bachelor's degree at Saginaw Valley State University and later studied in Mexico City. She taught school for a year in a U.S. State Department School in Torreon, Mexico and finished her thirty-year career in Chesaning, Michigan. She is pleased her first e-book, *My Michigan Summer*, is now available in paperback. Her second book, *Remembering Pop Pop*, is also published on Amazon. She is currently working on her third children's book *Dancin' With Great Grandma*. Rose spends winters in the Southwest and summers in Michigan. This allows her to be near all four of her grandkids.

A special thank you to Fred Arndt for his illustrations and help in putting *My Michigan Summer* together.

Rose (Rosalee) Klopf Tithof
rtithof@gmail.com

About the Illustrator

Frederick Arndt is an artist and illustrator. After retiring in 2005 from a successful career as an engineering executive in the automotive industry, he turned his interest to his love of art. He has designed a wide range of artworks including: sculptures, metal and wood wall art, Christmas ornaments, kitchen accessories, and illustrations. Frederick's works have been exhibited at the Palm Springs and Los Angeles Modernism Shows and shown in various publications including the New York Times and Chicago Tribune. His work is available at various locations across the country as well as on numerous websites including his Fred Arndt Artworks Etsy Store, Houzz, and Food52.

Frederick Paul Arndt
fparndt@aol.com

www.ingramcontent.com/pod-product-compliance
Lightning Source LLC
Chambersburg PA
CBHW041817040426
42452CB00001B/8